The Sky Is a Bird of Sorrow

The Sky is a Bird of Sorrow is an apt title for Steven Dieffenbacher's new book of poems. Like the sky, the scope of the poetry is wide, primarily a sweeping vision of spaces and eras specific to the West — Oregon, New Mexico, deserts, mountains, ocean shores, the land and its people. The tone of voice, maintained almost consistently throughout the book, is filled with the sort of longing that beauty and wonder always occasion. Loss and searching, treated honestly and straightforwardly through events human and earthly, are Dieffenbacher's major themes. "On the rim of the canyon/I have come to find you."

— Pattiann Rogers, author of *Wayfare* and *Generations*

These gentle, well-considered poems travel American landscapes of the domestic, historic, and prehistoric. In virtually every line, Steve Dieffenbacher celebrates the complications of human occupation and succession, always asserting the possibilities of a life well-lived: "if it be not now, yet it will come, our last and deepest love."

— David Axelrod, author of *What Next, Old Knife?*

From this poet whose German surname evokes a "deep stream" comes a collection both lit and shadowed from within by a Rilkean lyricism. Dieffenbacher gives us poems that can hear a *"...continent's breath/heaving out of distance/from plains of frost."* His is a gift capable of conveying the language of a wounded tree, its *"... aching, broken/top," its "...bell/of wooden bones."* Brimming with stunning tropes, alive with liquid music, his poems carry *"...the mute undertow of another earth."* On these pages, a fortunate reader finds language that reaches *"to the root of the world."*

— Paulann Peterson, Oregon Poet Laureate

When the geese call in late autumn, this book says, they call for you. Crossing borders, climbing the rim, holding a vigil at dawn, these poems forge elegy in each hour of each day, like birds graced with dark wings. In poems like these, even sorrow can fly.

— Kim Stafford, author of *The Muses Among Us: Eloquent Listening and Other Pleasures of the Writer's Craft*

The Sky Is a Bird of Sorrow

STEVE DIEFFENBACHER

La Grande • 2012

ISBN: 978-1-877655-75-3
Library of Congress Control Number: 2012932497

First Edition
April 2012

cover painting: "Loom of the Land"
title page: "Heaven and Earth," (see additional notes in back)
www.dongraystudio.com
Cover Design: Kristin Summer, www.redbatdesign.com
Interior Design: David Memmott
Author Photo: Deidre Dieffenbacher

Published by
Wordcraft of Oregon, LLC
PO Box 3235
La Grande, OR 97850
editor@wordcraftoforegon.com
http://www.wordcraftoforegon.com

Member of Council of Literary Magazines & Presses (CLMP)

Text set in Adobe Garamond Premier Pro
Printed in United States of America

For my wife Terry,
my children Deidre, Devin and Shannon,
and my brother Dennis

"Maybe we're here only to say: *house,*
bridge, well, gate, jug, olive tree, window —
at most, *pillar, tower* ... but to say them, remember,
oh, to say them in a way that the things themselves
never dreamed of existing so intensely."
— **Rainer Maria Rilke,** "The Ninth Elegy"

Acknowledgments

Some poems included in this collection appeared in the following publications, some in slightly different form:

"Emptiness," winner of the Cloudbank 2010 poetry contest, in *Cloudbank*
"Winter Under the Shadow of the Siskiyous," in *Deer Drink the Moon: Poems of Oregon*
"Table Rock Pilgrimage," in *Frame Houses* and *A Path Through Stone*
"The Ice of Love," in *At the Boundary*
"On the Cliff," in *Fireweed*
"Dark Places," in *Labyrinth: Poems and Prose*
"Night Singer, Chaco Canyon, New Mexico," in *Comstock Review*
"North Umpqua," in *Manzanita Quarterly* and *Universe of the Unsaid*
"Back from the Desert," "Love at the Equinox," in *Voices from the Siskiyous*
"The Echo of Small Birds," in *At The Boundary, JPR Monthly*
"After Her Surgery," "A Silent World," "At Taos Pueblo," "Commencement 1996: Ashland," "Falling," "Headwaters," "In the Moment in a Dark Wood," "Joy," "Late Autumn," "Lost in the Aleph," "Morning," "Parting: Love and Ashes," "Rain," "Storm, Bandon, Oregon," "Storm at Ghost Ranch, New Mexico," "To a Young Woman Reading," "The Sky Is a Bird of Sorrow," "The World in Black and White," "Waiting," "When Night Falls," "Undiscovered Country," "The Universe of the Unsaid," "White Midnight, Black Dawn," in *Universe of the Unsaid*
"Glacier Park, Night of the Grizzly, 1966," "Headwaters," "Machetes," Maybe," "The Ghost of Neanderthal Man Comes to Lascaux," "The Woman Across the Room," in *A Path Through Stone*

Quotations from Rainer Maria Rilke are from *Duino Elegies and The Sonnets to Orpheus,* translated by A. Poulin, Jr., published by Houghton Mifflin Company, Boston, in 1977.

The quotation from "Gilgamesh" in "Dark Places" is from *Gilgamesh Translated from the Sin-Leqi-Unninni Version,* translated by John Gardner and John Maier, published by Vintage Books, 1985.

My special thanks to the following, who made this book possible:

For invaluable help in the shaping of these poems, my fellow poets and friends, Jonah Bornstein and Vince Wixon, as well as my Friday and Saturday writing groups.

For her enthusiastic support and incisive comments about the tone and themes of key poems, Liz Nakazawa.

For his encouragement and permission to use his painting, "Loom of the Land" on the cover and the evocative drawings of birds starting each section, painter Don Gray. What I try to do in words he has captured in his art to set the ideal tone for this book.

For planting the seed of my return to poetry many years ago, George Venn, and for nurturing it afterwards, the late painter/poet Garrett Miller.

For making the creation of this book a collaborative process in the best sense of the word, Wordcraft of Oregon publisher David Memmott, for his understanding, patience, persistence, and attention to detail.

And for inspiring and honoring my devotion to this work, my wife, Terry, with love and gratitude.

Contents

Love at the Equinox

When Night Falls

Home Ground

The Sky Is a Bird of Sorrow

Love at the Equinox

Flyover, 2011

The Ice of Love

What we hear at night
under the grass
is the ice of love.
We who walk disconsolate
cannot follow these sighs
unless earth rises,
cannot cross the river
unless stones move.
We hear these groans
as the continent's breath
heaving out of distance
from plains of frost.
Under this belt
time is green and ancient,
the voice of water when ice
rushes out of mountains
to a gorge of flesh.

The Raven's Call

Must the sun rise saffron
when the morning bell
declares us naked and unborn?
When we join in the hour
before the shades burn
do we stumble out of shadows
just for a memory of light?
If we seem full in that moment,
one gaze across the table,
coppery in candlelight,
have we filled each other
only for a new emptiness?

In the morning before the clock strikes,
when the gray cock crows
its cold hour along the fences
it is my cells who call to you.
If my life has come to this,
if I am to greet the awakened hour
as an absence,
I must know you as nothing can be known,
a raven dark across the field
pursuing the echo of its own shape
from the beginning of time,
the one sure desire.

Morning

Trees speak
with their limbs.
Geese draw near
where water comes
out of foggy mountains.

Leaves hang
like frozen birds,
saying, "This way
and that," their words
braced with wounds.

What can I say
that isn't my wound, too,
an aching, broken
top, a bell
of wooden bones.

On the Cliff

Zion National Park, Utah, 1969

I stroke your arm
each time we turn
and look at the river
on the terrace facing west.

In that light past is present,
we seem more than we were,
the river clearer,
your hair brighter than pearl.
We climb the gray wall again,
feeling the rock,
seeing the colors of afternoon.
Did the sunset really come?
Did the stream run under our feet?

We move on cliffs
smaller than we knew,
until there is nothing left
but what we saw.
How could we know the day
would age like wine?
How could we know we'd turn mute?

Maybe

At the top the oak shudders.
She has stopped talking.
Maybe we came here together
fingering the wind, shivering.
Maybe we came separately,
unconscious of the cold
or the rain
coming from the mountains.
I see how she is like a cacao bean,
how her chin juts and the strands
of dark hair stream away from her.
She sees my eyes move with hers,
the suggestion of muscle
under my beard.
Maybe we stare at each other
with that gold look,
fusing like a gravitation
of two birds around a tree,
matching our wings
to the pulse of the mad sky,
kissing with all the tenderness of loss
beyond any idea of grace.

Maybe we only imagined the mountains
and are sitting across from each other
in our ranch-style house
looking into the yard,
eyes pressed into the roses pink against the fence
where the broken board
swings.
In this reality we only dream.
I can tell you she always came first,
meeting me by the manzanita at the edge

where we ate lunch often,
and that I followed
her footprints to the scarp
knowing her eagerness for love.
Now the rain comes straight at us
and the sky is venomous.
I see she is older, her hair flecked,
sinews like knotted madrone.
This time we stand apart from grace
certain of nothing
but what each wills the truth to be,
backing into the chaos
a simple touch dissolves.

Parting: Love and Ashes

Your eyes are the sea's hearts
four-chambered,
filled with caves.
I do not know them,
but I have seen them arc with light
in the vacant hours
when the tiger walks.
I have come with all my furniture,
my duties
sharp and startled at midnight
marching into the room
where candles stroke
our crushed flesh.
I smell the charred skin,
the residue of us
lifting to moonless dusk.

We do not kiss;
we glitter in bunks,
clinging to fences,
surrounded by hounds.
You tell me you will not rise
or dress again in stripes.
You will not stand naked
or reach your hand out of this clay.
No soldier can save you.
No wire can hold you.
We sit and talk until our sound
is only the idea of sound
and the universe swivels beyond us
to other voices
ardent and booming with stars,
spinning with joy.

Commencement 1996, Ashland

I want this to be what
I have told you it *should* be,
a night latent with meaning,
the trees leaning in stillness
over the platform
as you sit lantern-eyed
under the high cedar near the road.

There is so much I want to say.
That this may be the summit of hope,
that things will never turn out as you expect,
that you too may sit like me
missing the reed-thin echo
of your daughter
in a whirl of flitting moths.

Already summer voices echo across the grass,
saying *another season must come.*
On the blanket, your mother leans
into her lover and he
strokes her back, smiling at me.
When I take your picture
you are a wild toss of tassels
but I cannot help
holding you in that lens
more still and sharp than you can ever be.

"There's nothing out there," I say,
"nothing you could want,"
but your foot is already to the edge of the stage,
your gown billowing around you,
strands of red hair warming
to the chilly air.
Mouth open wider than my embrace,
you walk lightly into the dark.

Rite of Passage

The young men of the house
don't know who they are.
They have flowers,
they have trees
and the promise of gardens
but they walk in shadows.

They climb the mountains
with beating hearts
pawing at their own colors
until their silent mothers
will not touch them.
Only the earth hears them.
Only the earth speaks to them
when their minds are filled with wanting
and the dark halo of tears.

They've come so far to be human,
wandering over the plain
to the bruised shadow of the cliffs of paradise.
They know their moon is scarred and broken.
They know their fathers walked along this stream
for a thousand lifetimes,
following its silence,
following their own fathers
who left no path behind them.

Where are the footsteps their fathers wrote upon the mud?
Where are the hearts they found in wildness?
Where are the mothers who made them?

Table Rock Pilgrimage

She ascends in clear light,
this Maria, the color of dolor,
who came up from the border
through cholla,
past the slow helicopter with infrared eyes.

Here, her voice is a contralto
willing the limits of her poor son's hand
up stony slopes of oaks and leaves
she sings to, beating a path of new being.
She feels her power,
plucks the light to inclinations
she'd never had when gringos went mad
in the red room
in Juarez.

"Te quiero, te quiero," she'd said,
lying in the flow of their vacant sighs,
throbbing across the cloth until the lost hour passed,
passed as filtered light in hollows across her face,
while on her table, the brown virgin, Guadalupe,
spoke Nahuatl again on Tepeyac,
words that drove her across the line into this new world,
clean as a hospital,
where she scrubs the infirmary on knees
she's finally told to stand.

Fleeing the border, she formed the boy
in a barn near Indio with a stranger bartering a biscuit,
shaped him out of her own dark earth
and gave him the run of her breast.
Now he grips
a full-grown song of will stronger than her own,
bone-breaker cries that lead them up the hill like hawks
to gaze down scattered talus at the golden river,

here, where the sky glows like no sky in Mexico,
full of itself, whole,
and the mountains welcome the boy,
to set a table for their feast.

Headwaters

A nomad now,
autumnal
I wander below the mountain
turn from desert and stone,
my marriage of iron kisses.
All day through gray dust
my feet are clouds of pumice rising
under the gathering storm
a numbness of the broken land.

Then the sky becomes silent
and I know one rhythm only
of limb and grief
that moves into its own quiet
under the clatter of birds passing
over the white dead wood
until I pass with them
into the darkness of fir,
into the sound of voices
that are no more my foolish life moaning
but the sound of water calling.

I stand then
in fullness
as the water splashes
like milk
over the molding stones,
a whisper
of one man naked
returning at last
my call to water,
the source of the world
words of stone and mud.

The Woman Across the Room

I will not look into your eyes
or ask your name.
I will watch untouched
from the far side of the room
as you glide with your cup
along the door
filling yourself with shadow.
I'll trace your paleness there,
watching you lean
in the scent of gardenias,
believing again in lips.

Already I see your legs flying
over the hills
trailing their black silk
like the tango of a storm
I imagine from a great distance
in that doorway
where you watch with your cup,
and wait as I wait
and do not sing.

White Midnight, Black Dawn

This is the moment of terror:
She stands in the doorway
picking up the paper
after a night of sheets and sinew
deeper than my deepest song.
I see her face has changed
under the gray light,
no longer a half-line of shadow,
no longer haloed
as the day begins to edge itself jagged
over that candle fusion made
in a final, full outcry of rain.
I know I must make this walk alone,
all water and earth
to that starless dawn,
a loss so profound I cannot face it.
Was I finally pure
inside her?
Was I finally aware of shadow and light
when her white heart
sailed me speechless
on her tide?
Was I finally tired of wandering
through ashes and words
just as she closed the door
afraid we loved each other too much
under an indifferent sky?

Rain

Some nights rain cries
from a roof so uncaring
it calls for listening,
a dream of someone missing,
a hidden snakeskin
on a desert plain,
gates open to red sagebrush and cicada.
How the uncalled for, profound sandstone,
is such sweet pain
in the clear presence of rocks,
the dry canyon that falls into water,
a lizard's kiss out of the desert,
summoned only with trying.

Joy

In the nights of trees and storms
she is the last minute on earth.
She rises with light and subtle echoes,
she hunts me through sleep.
I wake, stretch my tired hands into a day
that cannot be a day without her.
At twilight, long past sighing,
beyond the cries we wanted to give,
we feel the scales of time judge us,
an ancestral fear in the throat of longing,
yet we still sing, returning to what we were.
We look at each other and wonder who we are,
but we dare not lose *this,* not *this.*
Sandpipers blow through us,
legs and mouths glide through our waters
and in the shadow of the morning we imagine a fish
out of the depths ready to die
just for the sight of us, the light we touch,
lips spread wide and full of tongues,
all our secret places.

Lovemaking

You want to believe in its transcendence,
a going out of this life
where sensation can only be
what lives in the hour of need.
It is what you wish your life to be,
every moment a whisper or a howl,
every act the god you might have made.

You want every day to build
and wane in the center of it,
a music that fills you,
this sudden everything that comes
from the loneliness you were born with,
that mewling, human fear
so large now you feel it
on your back, a wing
without flesh or voice,
taking all you have of heart and tongue
to give more than you deserve.

North Umpqua

All day light burned from the trees
and we longed to follow it
to the end of the canyon.
It was what lay before,
land and water
and the night's blind sound.
It was what our bodies comprehended,
what the stone was
when we bent out of reeds
toward the voice of water.
We heard what the stone said
and the water's answer
when we could say nothing to each other,
a torrent silent
in the act of falling.

After Her Surgery

"I'm not good at this," I tell her,
"this giving wholly to another."
Every morning I examine her scar
from back to stomach,
imagine the engorged kidney under it
untangled at last and draining.
I want to trace the cut folds
pressed into a grim insult,
but she will flinch and I cannot bear it.
This is the skin I once touched
as unblemished as alabaster.
It is what I remembered along the river
as madrones uncovered new green
under peeling bronze.
For a moment I think I am safe there with her
even as she turns to me
with the need and fear of that touch
I cannot pain her with.
I know the shrubs along the path
have turned raucous and vibrating
in a season that holds the earth
from dissolution. I try to believe this,
and I say it to her, but it seems like smoke
floating outside the window
where the hills have burst into flame
and the heartwood melts.

Scar

I tell her I want to lie beside her
to restore the muscle within.
I say her back is strong,
the shoulder blades woven
to stroke across still water.
The scar has turned white,
the half circle around her side a silver more beautiful
than the red around it, a gleaming canal.

The surgeon was deft with this cut, I say,
must have known the desolation
it would bring, grieved for it
and then cut on.
How firmly the membrane closes, I say,
how brightly it shines
with a life of its own, a corded ridgeline
I could lose myself in.

Storm, Bandon, Oregon

She wakes in the dark at four
to stare through the window at men
digging in the rain.
"How can they?" she asks.
"How can they work,
in that?"

All the men in the world must come here,
played out at the end of their lives
against this rock,
watching seals bark
in some call of stone.

Awake, we satisfy ourselves,
stretch chests and backs,
curl into each other
until our heads dangle wild
over the edge.
I dream, make an apple
out of thin air,
until she dreams, too.
I reach for her.
I weigh myself in her.
She weighs every word.
"Are men dead?
Why can't you just feel?"

Wind gathers its broken teeth around us.
Will the roof hold?
Can the men hold on?
Her fingers expand under my palms.
I lie over her,
and she sighs.

Beyond the mountains, the rain stops.
Beyond the ocean, voices fade.
Outside our window,
the gruff shouts of men
and a blare of foghorns
we choose not to hear
even as we join.

Love at the Equinox

In September, light seems truer,
and this would be enough for me,
but geese circle the gray nimbus,
strange winds trouble the waters.
If I stand in a city far from here
where streets are cobbled and September
moves along the water, don't I still hear bagpipes
when she is with me?
Doesn't the song's lament rise
as we touch those stones along the quay?
On the deck, islands move
and the sky recedes.
This is a perfect moment, she would say,
and I can only believe her
even as another night's advent hangs with shadow
and the red water carries us as far as we can reach
into the narrows.

Late Autumn

Now, there is nowhere to go,
and I know this is how it has always been.
I walk outside, and beyond the path, cottonwoods quiver,
geese call across the browning water.
This is *my* call, and they have come for me.
I drive north to the river I love most
and tell her she is the swift and brown-eyed woman
I see clearly at last even as she moves away
and says nothing. At her tallest waterfall, I look up
at maples and alders yellow with dying
and feel her shadows move in as I walk away
unhurried into the embers of my life
not stopping for a picture of where I've been.
Then the maples flare out. All I have
is a wheel in my hands, the memory of a river
red with autumn under the light of darkening pines
on this road to a place I call home,
filling so easily with night.

When Night Falls

Food Chain, 2011

Naked on the Beach

Puerto Cabezas, Nicaragua, 1955

I took my clothes off
and put them under the palms.
The docks were voiceless, the boats
already rocking out to sea.
Along the beach I walked
whiter than the sand,
whiter than the sun's words
of heat and color.
The coconut cutters waved.
The brown fishermen rowed.
The women swayed with their baskets,
turning to the sound of the sea.
I walked for hours beside the palms
in the horizon's white silence.
When my parents found me
I could not remember where I'd been
or where my clothes were,
or what the sea had said.

The Universe of the Unsaid

In the morning the man reads a book.
The book bends slightly in his hand,
the pages pressing against his flesh.
Through the window, mist trails over the plateau,
pines press against the sky.
His son comes out of the bathroom
and the man closes his book,
running a thumb along the spine.

All his life the man has felt a shiver
just beyond himself, clouds winging
along the precipice, runes pressing
through the same air his body moves through.
He thinks he knows this chant
as the shriek of the universe,
his own voice coming back to him
from the womb or the grave.

The boy looks at his father
and wonders why the man
cannot speak to him, remembers
how they walked into the hills behind the town
and built a bonfire against the fog,
a shrouded whisper of their loneliness.
He wants to tell his father
how the leaves seemed to hear him in the trees,
and how a sigh rose like a bird's wing
and seemed to touch him
and how when he turned, the air was quiet.
He sees his father looking at the clouds
pressed to the window and wonders
what the man tries to touch in that transparency
of air, palpable against the glass.

All afternoon, sleeves of fog come to the man
and he cannot stop thinking of how
his son emerged from the bathroom
scuffling over the rug.
Across the room, his son's picture
leans against a philodendron
that moves with the day's light
until at sunset the boy lies curled on the couch
under a blanket snoring.
The man thinks he hears the timbre of words
reverberating through the wall
and wants to reach through the window for them
but the sound recedes from him,
recedes as it always has when he leans toward it.
He turns back to his book,
bends the pages slowly, watching their creases give
under his weight as the boy sleeps,
until he sleeps, too.
They move into their farthest expanse then,
voices calling to them as they sleep,
until they roll through a river of air
and hear each other, crooning and solitary,
the only voices in the cloud.

Winter in the Shadow of the Siskiyous, Talent

It is hours past
the gray and white
morning's rise over stiff
starlings on voiceless wires,

the day a shroud
of dull silver behind blinds
blocking the language
of ascension.

All I can hope for
is sound, the bands
of late-afternoon mustard
resolving to jabbers,

evening's undernotes
after a month's rain
when all my hunger is for violet
over the mountains

and all I can summon
are the lost swallows of summer,
the uncertain hum in the air
of imagined sunsets

while sharp squares
of light rake the floor
here under the window
with a clarity I cannot direct

or resist, a forgotten
spectrum of blind luminance
equally shadowless,
just as indifferent.

The Reader

She faces some distance
words have brought her to,
her right hand relaxed slightly
over the book, where one page bends
in a last flicker of breeze.
Behind her, tendrils of leaves hang
in Chinese whirls,
luminescent and blurred
through a screen of water.

She already looks beyond
the life she has yet to live,
the golden hair spun
in a tangle of words
pearled and oysterless around her.

Beyond the leaves
a white mist rises,
She hears languorous water,
the mysterious syllables of birds,
her own tremulous voice
lifting slowly from the shore,
an echo of violet wings.

The Echo of Small Birds

All along the ridgeline, she senses them
in brush on stony ground,
a trail of pine and oak.
She can barely hear them,
turning only toward their faint calls
as she feels herself fade.
This is not what she has come for,
this severing of self,
this loneliness up a slope of stones.
She has only followed the path
she was meant for,
a rise clearly marked
and strewn with leaves.
All her life she has waited for something
to come over the horizon,
some blast of yellow or rust,
but nothing has come to her
except this bustle of wings
out of brush,
a breeze leaning into stillness,
some faraway hum.

Departure

You think it's a brief good-bye,
a lift of hand along the gangway
on a journey she's taken before,
a cruise south with friends,
but then she falls out of your life
as if she never existed.
You search every ship's manifest,
try to place what storm
took her out among the rocks
to a shore you secretly longed for.

You imagine her in Portugal
tracking across the long beaches
of a new continent, a place strange
and far away. You see her in a pine forest
across a lake-filled plain
asleep within a circle of trees,
or in the Caribbean
under scented mangoes,
a creature of the beaten sun
beside a blue, translucent sea.

You want to go there,
to leave quietly without farewell
from a world bitter with loss
to that place of dances where shapes rise green
into a pungency of murmuring voices,
where the one life flows inside you
out of windblown palms,
where all you have to do is walk
to know the meaning of breath.

At Fort Rock

On the path, my bootprints
head into bare land,
the straight way
through mottled scrub into far hills.
Here, the fortresslike walls erode,
alone with sage and desert grass,
frayed sandals in a cave.

Once there were lakes and prairies,
patches of forest,
men who sat beside a fire
eating bison and camel.
Today lonely eyes roll across silence
to a growing line of shadow
that cuts the hills in half.

The Hunter

At Hart Mountain, Oregon

Birds cried under the rim as he stood
in that reach of twilight sky
stretching to blue mountains.

Stalking the tall grass, atlatl in hand,
he gazed at dying lakes, the receding woods
turning to tans and sunset yellow, a steady dust.

At the lake, I scrabble through sage
seeking him in lichen, scraped shapes of animals
where the unyielding stone cuts

through dry branches above
the graying shore, try to become him
moving toward rims beside shallow water.

There, his handiwork climbs still —
a painted turtle thin-legged and pale
marking a mottled way from earth to sky.

I see him and his kinsmen silent as he paints,
backs hooded under rock as I walk away,
grateful for anything that can still be hidden.

The Ghost of Neanderthal Man Comes to Lascaux

He comes into the cave
as I stand on the ledge
with the stone bowl
red with ocher,
not seeing his ridges
lost in shadow,
the arms heavy with hair.

I lean like a dancer
into the wall,
brushes forming deer
along this rock
with a brain so finally human.

My torches burn
but he still comes
a shadow across my brow,
moving out of my past
fainter than any breath
of ice and snow
of graves so deep
they shape this ground.

Hold your hand up like stone,
fan the fire inside our circle,
find the axe inside the rock.
Walk here inside me,
come from my shadows
and I will hold you.
Tell me who we are.
There is still time.

Death of the Iceman

In that moment
he is checking something,
perhaps one of the unfinished arrows
or the fine copper ax,
his symbol of authority.
It is spring, but still cold
in the Alps, the wind rising.
He thinks he is safe now,
thinks he has outrun them
as he stands near the pass.

Earlier, in the forest,
seeds had whirled around him,
hornbeam flakes
in fragmentary sunlight.
He paused there first,
washing his hurt hand in the stream,
and climbed on.

Now, on this ledge,
he puts his grass cloak down,
holds the quiver in one hand,
looking at the mountains,
sensing snow.

Then from the rocks
a crack of footsteps
as he begins to turn,
falling into glacial twilight,
those centuries of waiting
with an arrow in his back.

The Yde Girl

I

On the day of sacrifice,
she stands over the pit,
a cold wind and unseasonable snow
lacing her naked shoulders.
She says nothing
into the gray hills.

What is she thinking
as he holds the knife at her throat?
That the year had been dry,
the harvest barren
and she willing to die?
Or do her eyes dart in terror?

Imperfect, her spine arcing
like a ragged half-moon,
she looks to the delicate grasses
at her feet, but her ivory skin,
bare to the waist, glistens
when the stroke comes.

II

Why does she haunt us?
Others were found with bones
softened within leathered flesh,
fingernails gleaming
in loosely clenched hands,
their backs like seams of bronze.

But she is grotesque,
a single tooth arching away
from a blood-dry mouth,
the burnished rope collaring

her neck under a tender drift
of pollen in faded eyebrows
with a stare that is hers alone,
and knows nothing of our fear.

Glacier Park, Night of the Grizzly, 1966

The four new girls,
the summer crew,
must have looked at each other
in that intractable quiet,
in the faint lowing whisper
of the just-cold air
as the sky's light
struck her like a scar,
her, the fated one,
who may have believed it was just watching,
was even a benevolent eye.

She opened herself then
to the twilight,
the gloom wheeling around her,
just her,
and for a moment she sighed,
must have,
in the wonder of it
the sky's dimming sparks,
that sheet of sequined light.

The bear scent sudden upon her,
she reeled out of her dream
as the first slash
peeled her skin,
the sheer grunting bigness
of him
uncompromising and feral
on her,
unrolling layer upon layer of skin
with each swing
white and red to the whiteness
again, of bone,
and then, when the zipper jammed

trapping her,
amniotic, fecal and screaming
in that bag,
dragged her over the ragged ground
sky-glint of stones half-eaten,
she gave him
everything she had,
her dream of a cafe in Paris,
the slow touch of the Frenchman
she had not yet met,
the sudden tightness
of her womb long past due.

Machetes

They cut cleanly through plants,
making the green creepers, the fleeing lianas
fall like streaks of giant rain.
The blade is wide for the broad arc
of a walker's swing
against those impossibilities of growth
at the continent's center.
This is what the tool was made for,
a way into the pastures
beyond the trees.

It is not for us
to know how the blade meets bone
far beyond the place where our lives move.
It is not for us to know how the body falls
when embraced by gravity
after the metal's swing.
It is not for us to know
how much red makes the steel rust
when it whirls again and again
through our cells.
We are only human against this solidity,
cradling our hardness inside,
letting the marrow whine against the edge
when reason fails.

Vapors rise in the green mountains
of Rwanda.
Plants breathe freely
under the African moon over the lakes
of Rwanda.
Heat rises over the abandoned fields
of Rwanda.
Do not look.
Only the people are dying.

I am so tired of remembering
this swing of the dead.
Just let me die, I say,
before the last good heart
drowns in blood,
before the water burns red,
before all our names are smoke
and all our children are dust.

We are nothing but the earth's own breath
returning.
Our vapors must come over the green mountains also.
The sky is powerless
and the swing of the blade
cannot be stopped.

War in the Desert

The white dormers are flung down,
the vined and rosy arbors
hang shattered and burning.
Soldiers tighten their bootstays
in the hours of darkness
to the squeal of metal.

In courtyards and towns,
all is a shock-lit landscape.
Listen, the books and shops are burning
with cries of broken glass.

We stand under tamarisks
in the desert.
We stand in hot rain
with the sound of lamentation.
We spread sage over the dead;
we remember
the songs of children
over the open graves.

Storm at Ghost Ranch, New Mexico

Over the Pedernal
clouds darken,
brujas sweep across
violet earth; life
bristles with sufferance.
This morning, coyotes hid
under a gentle sun, the air was still.
Now, distance
is theater, loves
of a lifetime hang by a cord,
words fight with despair,
desolation drowns
in thunder,
giants grab
for bloody rock;
even they can't find
purchase here, fading
like thought
into the heart of the storm,
the tracks of their nails carved
on the cleansing plain.

Afternoon Thunderstorm, New Mexico, After Hurricane Katrina

Here, no horizon low enough
to imagine a sea, only more clouds,
each mesa outside the window
singing of drought
and the hope of rain.
The lament of cottonwoods rolls
from every tongue in corrals of rock,
a loss to live by as the concrete islands
of New Orleans sink into the sea.
Here the good and swift Jemez comes
after every day turns black,
panting behind thick-set trees
an exhalation of mounting winds.

At Taos Pueblo

A stream divides the town;
turquoise doors are shut against the sun.
In the heat's undercurrents,
adobe fades into a tan dog.

Dust muffles footsteps
under a sky coiled blue and gray;
the sacred mountain
lies flat in midday light.

On a roof, a man holding a trowel
stops, headband dark with sweat,
looking toward the north.
What does he see there?

The Sangre de Cristos,
whose shadows flow like black birds,
move with the sky. Under them,
the mud walls rise brown and stark.

On a bench, under a tree,
time is the only offering.
Tourists take pictures
of the plaza in grave silence.

No open doorway
into the world's heart
speaks to them. The afternoon sky
stretches; the ground shifts
in a coil of wind.

When Night Falls

After Sept. 11

Stonehenge burst into blackbirds
and we saw it go.
Now we hoard all we have,
move into secret camps,
bury our provisions in graves.
I look at you
and we consume each other
in a loss of words.

This is the cosmology of fear.
We look at each other,
and there are no stories to tell.
This was the last word, we say.
Animal sounds lie about us.
We clatter our sticks against stone,
and when we wake,
there is nothing to heal.

On the rim of the canyon
I have come to find you.
The wind is cold.
My hands are chalk.
Under the edge, the sun falls
suddenly into night
and you are nowhere to be found
even as I call to you.

I am here, I say;
I will rebuild our fire.
Come and I will tell you
a story we both know,
the one about the river that angled
steeply through rocks.
I see it now.
It is the voice of color,
the light of the plateau
bending to the arc of the river,
waking without sound.

Falling

In this dream my brother is always
falling
toward a thin-thread bridge,
cables of lacewing nets over
black water.
I know it is only a dream,
even when he accelerates and fades as I arc
with him
past the black-white orb
of a gull's head.
The span above is held firm with steel
but he is a plumbline driving past
all diving birds
that bring the universe down, the
Greenland slabs of ice, the quake-
ridden Asian shores,
beach-black with fallen trees.
He plunges
and spins as if to unload all
the sounds of ice and sand
to help us fear less
so we can condense and drift
to those low Pennsylvania hills
we walked
that autumn before our father died,
those hills recast now
into a green, spring backdrop
behind the mound where he pitched
to my perfect batter's
arc beyond the cabin in that field where
my father stands in my dreams before he
falls like my brother
is falling into this great and ruined sea.

Undiscovered Country

For my father, b. 1917, d. 1962

In a white farmhouse
I wake and call
to my father.
"Am I going to die?" I say.
My father waits for an answer.
"We all have to die," he says.

The wings of the desert lift me
into white November hills
beyond a road
of twisted leaves
in the grip of fall.
Storms brew
over the empty town.

Does wind become water?
Does air shape earth
as the voices of the living echo the dead?
On the scarp
the air is fresh and cold.
A waterfall
rushes out of stone into a basin,
pushing itself over the plain.
Across the river, a pelican flies
toward an unseen lake,
its wingbeat the weight
of my dream.
Rock spills into sand;
sand turns to stone.
A lizard comes out of rock,
and speaks in the voice of my father,
eyes shining like amber
on a shore of bone.
"Am I going to die?" he says.
I wait for an answer.

Home Ground

The Memory of Moisture, 2011

Home Ground

Mother, I always wanted to tell you
that the clouded moon is like a distant rain
or feathers across the dark,
that the touch of skin is a drum that plays the heart
on hills the nights forget.

Across the wires, our words crack.
Why did I leave?
You must know.
On the tarmac you embraced my new wife
and said, "Take care of him."
You couldn't let go.

You come north now,
find yourself in Oregon,
gold leaves under your feet,
the sweep of a storm across the valley.
We talk and watch my children
smile and lift their wings.

At night we sit in your motel room
drinking slow rum and coffee, old movies
flickering across our screens.
Words form between us.
We are suddenly strong with words.

You look as you always did,
raven-haired, dark queen, a love of knowing smiles.
I did what you asked, measured time slowly,
touched others in layers as careful as yours.
But oh, how you laughed
in those old letters from Peru.
"How the men liked me," you tell me now,
"as your father dug copper from the earth."

This morning, your head leans,
your shoulders bend in a surprise of snow,
gray raincoat wound tightly around you as we walk.
Maybe then you were too much the admiral's daughter.
Maybe my voice was too strange and lonely
and my wife the only ear that would listen.

Now she is gone and you endure.
I know I followed your tracks into the shape
of what I am, fresh sounds beating between us
through these Oregon hills, what once was hard
thawing slowly, still unsure of its ground.

Leavetaking

Chula Vista, California
For my mother, b. 1920, d. 2009

I was never at peace there,
but every day was pulled into a maelstrom
of pealing horns and hammered music,
the empty stone and glass fronts grating
in always purposeful mornings
as people streamed to face the town, all wind.
One day as I walked beside them I saw a man
holding a woman by a strap across a street
while she stood howling, pacing fiercely,
eager to leap into the beaming crush of traffic,
while the man yanked the strap tight
until she cried and tried again.

Some days, I thought I saw the beauty
people had fled here for,
the yellowing sky of palms licked by ocean breezes,
the clear gold in morning bays stretched toward blue
buildings that woke into a radiance
that glowed day-long with lingering colors
far from Midwest ice and Eastern snow
as I waited for the hour I would sit with my mother
in the small room her life had become.

There, I gazed from a second-floor window
as she lay back, mouth wide,
a sleeping bliss through TV crimes that made
their way into me, a lurid, nightmare body
where more of me disappeared every day, slivers
fading from tangible, thick-toothed spines
of maguey below the room as I read of distance
in the chair beside her, New Mexico's osier ridges
and summer storms a desperate remembrance of change.

One afternoon I drove her east
out of the city beyond the palmettos

and careful grass where houses came to a terminus
of brush and dark-brown soil,
bare hills rising into a cloudless sky,
an emptiness stretching to redeem
all that had been lost. Then the pain returned,
her bent spine a mute anguish,
her shoulders no longer able to hold themselves
to any fierce resolve. I reached for her then,
patted the thin, clenched hand on her lap
to hold in the pain and turned the wheel
from my own will back to the houses keeping
the raw teeth of everything wild at bay.

That night in my motel I awoke to the thunder
of drums from passing cars, and rose to look
into the bathroom's frosted glass where streetlights
blurred yellow through a window I couldn't open
even for a taste of morning before going to her,
remembering the trees and fog
of a more familiar loneliness, the birds and beating
rain of Oregon, where my own life called
even in the grief of the dying year.

"I hate to see you go," she said that night,
the long hall stretching behind us
after food in the light of her flickering screen,
her eyes searching mine for a will as strong as her own
to meet the desolation to come.

In the morning I drove through vacant streets,
rushing to the airport where every retreat
banishes regret, the city's cargo of guilt falling back
into its sleeping, crowded stares and shoulders,
my relief clearer with each mile on sun-swept wings
even as what I could not say echoed and haunted me,
"I'm afraid I won't be strong enough to let you go,"
imagining her bent head rising in that room she hated
knowing she would hold on silent to the end
and that no look or touch could ever release us.

In Bed with Blood Clots, Remembering the San Juans

I begin every day dizzy,
a half-reckoned equator
because death seems only death
when the mind begins to die,
all nerves a fading August light,
a cooling gust in leaves
losing their gladness early.

The meaning of time is in everything,
bending flowers in a garden like an old man's stoop,
a porch's flaking paint like a woman's rasp of skin,
angled light through windows
another day's exhaustion.

All morning the cats linger on rugs
like small, bony horses dying,
joints cracking in a swiveling sun
under my mother's picture, a half-amused smile
that already knew too much of loss.

Every day her grandchildren smile beside her,
three uplines of hope
while behind them
the silent harbor waits
as evening mist grows.

Eight months after she died, no one beside her,
I recline with blood in my lungs
wait for what time wants,
recall the islands, the moment
when she posed and looked happy,
the morning I went outside for blackberries,
and found none.

Losses

The ashes sit in a tin smaller
than a coffee cup, grains of dust
so airy they could float away.
Will she come to me in dreams,
the green, star-burst pupils
and black-mask face?
She slept curled, a feline nest
listening as I walked,
rising only to wait, paws together
until even that was too much
for her emerging bones.

One night I looked at her,
and dreamed of my mother,
the unyielding presence of my boyhood,
made mute in a nondescript room
far from me, too quick for summoning.
"They have work to do
on the other side,"
my cousin said softly at the funeral.
"Then they come back and visit you."

Two weeks ago, my father's sister sent
a picture of him during our last autumn,
he, my mother and brother in a line of relatives,
all dead now, on grass under heavy trees.
On one side, my brother, adolescent and sure stands;
on the other, I at 12, smile
into the Pennsylvania afternoon
as my mother sits,
uncharacteristically relaxed,
smiling, too, in the foreground.

I imagine my aunt wrapping the prints
in notepaper, writing that some were faded

from the Susquehanna flood
after being dried in the sun.
"I'm 91 now," she writes, "and thought
you should have these."

Across the dun hills outside,
snow again. White land, white sky.
Fifty years ago I stood before the world, smiling;
here an Oregon winter falls
in drifts of sameness.
The tin sits on this table,
painted paw prints like dark metal
glare under this dim inside light.
How strange. A cat sleeping
her life away across this room,
a presence hardly recognized
until she was gone,
to bring this all back.

In Chaco Canyon

In the flaying sun, my friend does not like the warning,
"Area Closed Beyond This Point," the only sign of life here.
For him every sign is a barrier against winds he would summon
to hold his spirit in against a fear of blowing away.

He wants, he thinks, one mother tongue to know him,
some finality of movement under butte-washed sunsets
as he walks red ground accompanied only by shadow,
unfixed in the desert's slow dissolve to the sea.

He fears a life without yearning, seasons of stone riveted
to iron, unable to move ahead or back beyond
an emptiness of arroyos and indefinite skies hung
like cloth on mesas while dust swirls faithless around him.

Behind us all seems blue; before us, substanceless
reaches of brush and cloud inviting delusion.
They may be real; they may be true as only desert lovers
believe them true, distances untranslatable and fatherless.

No being speaks to us here, no atmosphere of perfection comes,
only a sense of the departed. Rocks lean, the wind-blasted walls whistle,
the wash bends its arid furrows of lost water across a plain
of old roads where memories sleep and we stand restless.

Night Singer, Chaco Canyon, New Mexico

Your voice comes out of firelight at the far end of the campground,
an irresistible wind etched in moonlight along the cliff.
All day you crossed the dirt road for water or sat still at the table,
holding yourself in, "a Pueblo descendant," I say to my friend,

nodding toward your dark body as he nods back.
Now I cannot see you, but feel your breath stir as stars stream
like froth over us. I wonder how it is to be alone among strangers
in your own land, your voice all that colors a land you no longer know

until it is nothing but sound. I know you have a life different
from what I make of it, a clerk, perhaps, in Jemez Springs
who lingers in abandoned ruins to force a daytime grace,
refusing to answer the consonants of nearby foreigners

razoring the air. But now they are gone, My friend and I walk close
as you lie unmoving in the sun watching birds sway among rocks.
In the afternoon we drift near your tent, study the quiet ground
and screen of trees, gaze briefly into a cave just yards away,

and turn back. That night, moths hover around our lanterns as we sit
quietly with our coffee, writing a country of words in the quiet
until your lament returns to us, calls of an unknown language
shadowing the frail moon, unhurried and wordless.

Waiting

Taos, New Mexico

It is morning. The air is clear. I stretch
toward the plain, the swing
of birds under a calling sky, the knot
of language distilled to *yes* and *loss.*
Shadows hang over the Sangre de Cristos.
All is still. This moment,
this *ahora,* is the breath *of piedras de la tierra,*
stones of the earth rising in the hope of rain.
Over the hills, day takes its sweet time,
but no rain comes.

What good does it do to think
under so much sky?
Moon announces night, the violet of departure
closes in, a relief from longing.
Let this indigo gather, the darkening cumulus
of twilight that stretches into silence.
Aqui soy. Es todo lo que necesito.
All I need is here. I exist in loss,
hungry always
for the food of waiting.

Into the Heart of Stone

I want to be stone, here where time
stretches into the fractures of cliffs
and resistance bends to the hard bone of the desert.
I yearn for surrender,
imagination ripening into the decay
of a passing sky that is everything
I can grasp of the unknowable.
I imagine the stillness of canyons
as a final excavation of the soul,
desire absorbed into the ache for water
where boulders burn with more than heartbreak
because there is nothing to mourn and no one to mourn it,
but these spreading cracks louder than veins.

Desert Dream

I take her to my favorite
place — the pinnacles
where I'd first felt the call of stone.
I approach them slowly, stepping
across sand, wanting her
to feel the minarets, their bones widening
through her into a new body.
They seem to come for us
as we draw near, rocks emerging from themselves,
fissures groaning under the weight
of boulders no longer huddled,
but exhaling from the cliffs.

I lead her through ocotillo along terraces,
show her the datura's
yellow core and waves
of belled penstemons
along creases of seeps.
We walk through yucca
along washes where clouds stretch
in ligaments over us,
silence entering us as we walk.

I show her soil and fallen needles,
the gnarled arches of juniper,
the imprint of our own footsteps
wandering in uneven arcs across a broken land.
We hear a grasshopper, the clack
of its shadow lifting into scented air
an imminence of beating wings. Twilight comes.
We stand over a gray plumage of grasses
watching the last colors sweep the plain
with a longing we cannot unearth to each other,
dusk rising in us with the hot
slate outpouring of the desert
we no longer have to summon.

Back from the Desert

Something had already changed
as the two of them walked,
the language they'd spun,
missing something,
the world they'd come back to,
too lush and green,
its northern light
too faint and clouded.
They stand by their cars,
uncertain and awkward,
their smiles reduced
to a weariness of remembering
all that had sent them forth.

They tried to recall the radiance
of shale and turquoise that had rewarded
their promises
to unearth themselves.
They think of *he* and *him,*
instead of *I* and *you,*
and they cannot put their arms around
each other as they had on outcroppings
under the desert sun.
Their sadness is inexpressible.

For a moment more, they linger,
their despair as common to them now
as that joy inside the canyons
when they followed the flight of ravens.
A woman walks by and glances
toward them, and they look back,
noting the brown and backswept hair
the curious *yes* of her eyes,

the bare ankles reminiscent of noon
even on these streets swept by rain,
and they look at each other, finally, for an answer
to restore the arid sirens
they once conjured up everywhere
with a purer lust.

Dreaming of Crazy Horse

No Lakota knew where he went
in those days alone
when their world lay in shadow.
They imagined him in secret caves
or sitting on pale bluffs
watching windblown grass.

Once, near the end, he told them
he'd waited in breaks above the river,
so a wall at his back
could reflect the fire's heat.
That night an old man came
out of whirling snow,
recounting the old days
when buffalo walked
and dreamers spoke
in thunder.

In the morning he rose
to a cold, clear light,
the old man gone
with the snow.
He mounted his warhorse
and rode into grass,
nothing but distance before him
and the river's gash.

At the Little Bighorn

How bare the land was.
Hardly a sagebrush to hide behind,
rifle pits hollowed from resistant earth.

Today, from the last hill, a sea of buffalo grass
winds to the curling river's
narrow haven of trees.

Beyond, where the Indian village stood,
farmland and a mute freeway,
then spare, unrolling plains.

Under this cloudless sky, signs of the clash
wheel over wind-scoured miles,
headstones tracking the disarray.

Here, they made a stand, then moved on.
There, they broke, leaving their dead
in clay that couldn't hold blood.

To the south, the far Wolf Mountains
stretch blue across illusory space,
some direction they may have looked for
out of the smoke, a history already beginning to blur.

Chief Joseph Mountain

They named this mountain after him.
You can see his beloved valley from here,
but the trail stops short of the top.

He faces Mount Howard, uneven and forked,
named after the one-armed bluecoat
who wouldn't let him go.

A tram rises there all summer to trails
and a restaurant where you can gaze
back at him, gray-lined with late snow.

On clear days, his craggy blues lighten
late into a pale sky, become one with it,
unlimited, featureless.

Hells Canyon After the Nez Perce

For them it was home,
a place of fish and deer,
warm in winter.

Today the high cliffs hear little
but wind and swaying hawks,
a slow concourse.

Today we never stay long,
half the river, the misnamed Snake,
now too still behind our dams.

Too alone to look, even for them,
in this judgeless air,
we sit dumb in a house of echoes.

The World in Black and White

This is how I would make it,
tones that never fuse into a body,
nothing that ever moves toward anything
but itself. Just the drama
of shadow on stone, curving, perhaps,
into plateaus and waterless arroyos,
an uninhabited country
with low plants as still as rocks,
empty roads rolling their asphalt sheets
into clouds frozen white and gray
below the face of a blurred sun
that gazes colorless
at charcoal cliffs, a shining river.

Emptiness

We loved each other
to fill the emptiness,
conjugated the patterns of clouds,
danced to the voices of children.
At night we looked through windows
at stars and imagined them hot with being,
and this gave us some comfort
when we held our babies close and sang to them.
We tried to grasp this emptiness
in both hands and mold it to our hearts.
We saw it ripen with possibility,
the full pulp of the peach,
even as its outline was all we remembered.
Year by year we watched the fibers lengthen
around echoes of a seedless core.
And so the days rolled over us
toward the blackest colors we'd known,
the plants bursting with buds,
turning to creases in a cobbled road.
We lived in our uncertainty then,
an earth relieved of mounds,
the crystal black and white of winter,
the small sound of the bell.

The Sky Is a Bird of Sorrow

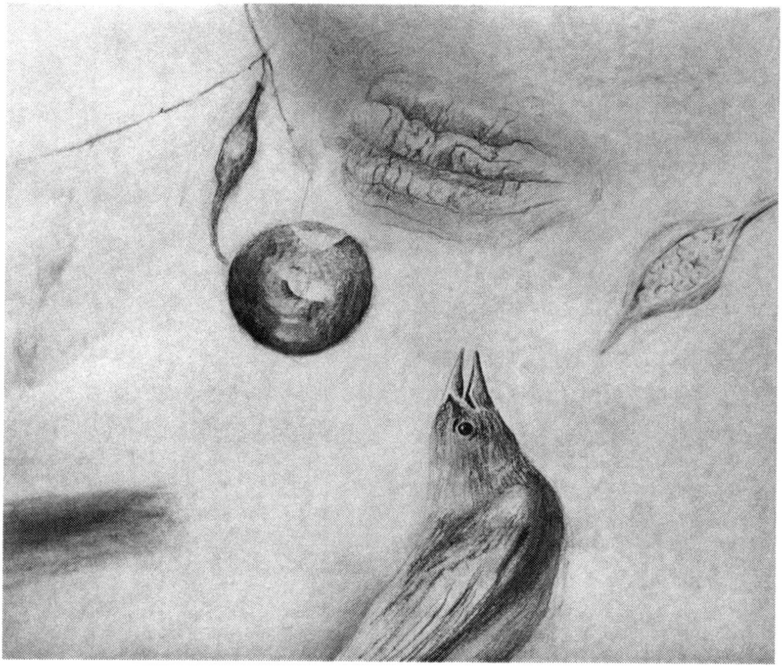

Season's Lament, 2011

The Sky Is a Bird of Sorrow

In time, he could only speak to her in dreams.

He saw the dry rivers
as he slept with her,
palm to her back
touching the echo of furrows
in her breathing.

He saw bats dying in webs of light,
snakes bleeding in mountains lost to him,
and wanted to walk above the sound
of their sorrow into vines and orange butterflies.

"Las mariposas, las mariposas,"
he said, trying to raise her in his dream.
"I was in a place of butterflies,
and their wings were like black pearls."
He did not believe she heard him,
but believed she whispered to him as he slept,
"I want tranquility
and you are the bird of shadow."

He looked for tranquility in his dream,
green and red shutters on a bay
whose windows opened to air
strung with the breath of fruit.
He saw fishermen's boats tilting on the sand,
a rush of insects, a rolling sea
and the bird of shadows lifting from the trees,
green above a river he'd followed inland
through violet and amber stones.
He rose from her sleeping body, then,
to yellow light and the smell of salt,

crooning the morning song he'd written
to her as he'd slept with crossed arms,

"El cielo es un pájaro de lágrimas,
y soy el pájaro de sombra.
The sky is a bird of sorrow,
and I am the bird of shadow."

Dark Places

After reading Sylvia Plath

Take care, Gilgamesh ...
Do not let your hand touch the waters of death ...
— "Gilgamesh"

I want to go there
because it speaks to me,
that dark center
where fear
and truth contend.

I follow her,
the animal cry of the woman
slipping me into water
no hand has touched
and lived to tell about.

I will do anything to get there,
anything in that tumble of rocks
where all voices rise
as if she and only she
could show me the way
with *yes* and *yes* and *yes*.

I feel her darkness
and believe her fear
more than a child's cry.
Nothing seems true,
nothing more real
than her mind's imprint
on scars of stone.
I see lilies
in next summer's pastures,
a river's gray water
retreat into the past
and how the lies of my own myths

settle like bowls
on my shoulder
their cumulus of false wounds.

I see what will kill me,
those symptoms of madness
dredged out of furry ground
and flung into life
from my what-have-beens.

With her beside me,
I tear at time,
mourn the one bent flower
and ravaged feathers
scattered in the garden.

I see how it can end then,
how the silent rage for the word
can go wrong,
how I would follow
the boom of her oar too far,
secrets I thought I might die for,
if I could only come back.

Lost in the Aleph

The Aleph: a point in space where all of existence can be experienced at once

By the time Borges's character found it
in a basement at the foot of the stairs,
he didn't know it would hurl him into chaos,
an endless, engulfing film, and he, the white
screen it played upon, a prisoner of history.
But what if you *could* take it all in and live,
see the furious, scarlet stars wheeling round
a plaid tablecloth in 1864 Petersburg
while the massive Yankee mortars boomed.
What if you *could* see Galileo staring into the gulfs
with that first telescope while a cockroach
slipped easily out of the tile under his foot?
What if you *did* carry the sweep of the Plains
in that restless loner checking traplines
as Allah and Jesus stood near their barren kings
and Tu Fu walked beside you quiet in an Asian twilight?
What would hold longer than a moment
in that swirl of image, sound and smell?
The birth of your first born, the concentrated
ring of cymbals from a Louis XIV orchestra,
the sweetness of an Appalachian spring
ripe with meadowlarks and the scent of berries?
Or for you, just for you, one small lizard
waiting in the desert beside a silver streambed
as ravens swooped over a bite of sage?
Would you know instantly where the water derives
its thunder out of canyons,
running through unresisting stone
to the far salt of the sea? Could you wait miles upriver
as the sky caught fire and fell into twilight
while your forefathers reeled out of their past,
meat slung across their backs,
presenting it to you as you sat by the flame?
Would it be enough to sit and watch time flee

back into the First Cause blasted instantly into details
of stone and fern, cactus and turquoise
as you looked into a pre-Cambrian sky
of smoking volcanoes and trilobite seas?
Or would you fix on the belches of cities,
customary Masses in Gothic cathedrals,
walks to work in gray dawns where dull streetcars
of the present wait for your footsteps to rumble
down a stairwell into the daily sway of subways
rolling toward the dark, final face of God
where the Aleph finally begins to fade and you stand facing
black windows under a weight so unbearable
you can see nothing? Would you wish then just to be
in Borges's basement again, waiting only for the sudden
crack in the door so can you run back
into your one, ordinary life?

The Incalculable

It, this namelessness, is beyond our science and our arts,
because its secret is being, not saying.
— John Fowles, "The Tree"

Even chaos has a theory and this is it — a summer wood is the sum
of wordlessness amid squawking jays while indelible, blind roots
plunge steadily downward. No touch can change it, this story of bark
too rough to sleep against, of leaves limp in midday's deluded blue.

This is a place where limbs bend too soon under the sky, bare survivors
aware of space's black carapace, that sure, unknown death,
while riverside stems burn and behind them fleeing rats get swallowed.
Even stars, their hydrogen furies breaking from each night's
checkerboard could be eaten by their own gravities or swell mad
in sudden confoundments of heat — novas reddening the face of heaven.

Meanwhile in Texas a scientist holds a stone knife, crude, barely triangular,
not Clovis, he says. In his hand, the tool of a new history starts
and another falls away, the old dioramas of hunters crossing a land bridge
melting — there was no way across when this tool was made.

Now, another story, a migration of boats along the ragged Pacific coast,
mariners reaching Channel Islands that today are the abandoned
reaches of fossils, relics of a spare human habitation and crying birds.
Yet in mainland deserts, where seas once flowed, the New Mexican rocks
sing of Kokopelli, the ubiquitous flute player, and of ripples like water
painted or etched in concentric circles shrinking toward a small dot.

There the door to another cosmology opens, magellanic clusters
that draw you in, caves with folds mysterious enough to be spoken to.
Years ago I sat facing an underworld's slow bulges, the desert behind me
as I inhaled whitened stone, pulled suddenly into the incalculable.

How long before I breathed again after that gasp of unknown power?
Today I walk among trees carrying mysterious cargos, my body shouting
a forgotten tongue, unreckoned gatherings that enter me through
dark stone, spiritless, large, listened to without a question.
In today's noonday sheen, only the cast-off gods rule. Living branches
hang spectral as I move in chaos — canopied, small, limitless.

Thorn

And if I cried, who'd listen to me in those angelic orders?
... beauty's nothing but the start of terror we can hardly bear.
— Rilke, "The First Elegy"

This was the cry revelation asked for and then gave,
the thrust into a hand that was pushing all known lives away
through winter-bare, berryless stems to glimpse the waiting mirror —
languid trees in a river's shadow, elongated hemispheres of light.

Beyond the tangle, water moved, ripples white and unheard
along half-drowned, bleached logs and midstream mounds of grass
for a truth that lay beyond. But then a sudden barb, a hand
trembling and retreating, and now this long, unhealing wound.

This is how devotion is rewarded, burning weeks of flesh too biting
for reflection while memories of shoreside plants rise from hints
of mute shadow to enter wordless into bone. For weeks,
the torn slit shouts, needle holes darkening the ears of sorrow.

And then, at last, some thin veil comes, slow-growing film
around a pain that breaks every night's peace. There the skin glows,
unknowing, new, covering all it learned of glassy dusk
standing at the mirror in phantom silence, aching and unsealed.

Deep Stream

Always facing creation, all we see
is the reflection of the free and open
that we've darkened ...
— Rilke, "The Eighth Elegy"

Brown branches and naked brush are inked water.
Only the mind remembers these reflections of itself,
the body puzzled away like Braque guitars, our grasping oneness
turned to quadrangles and broken frets of sound,
gazing back antiphonal at the death glimmers
of Narcissus — his moving song of water a thing of rock.

"Dieffenbacher, *yes, deep stream*", a German once said to me,
as we looked down together at a bird's writhing shadow.
Near us all was amber, the bare tops of rushes lifting like candles,
reaching down even then, I might have said, *to the root of the world.*
Yes, these depths still run clear in us while people die transparent
and otters call to us like monks from the deep — mirrored and fathomless.

Sea Change

Every angel's terrifying. Almost deadly birds
of my soul, I know what you are, but, oh,
I will sing to you!
— Rilke, "The Second Elegy"

These are the birds along the sea's horizon,
where glimmers of waves meet blue-gray lines
of clouds as indistinct as my life, the sun long gone
in its orange afterglow and final purples,
froth graying into twilight, infinite and beckoning.

I lie in a hospital room, wired to machines, blood drawn,
reduced to images — x-rays — the body's ghosts, remembering.
"Every angel *is* terrifying," I believe, and this, the most terrible
remains when the mind carries all, singing faintly
above every possible leaving — yours and mine.

Days later, curtained and alone, I dream of a woman underwater
and make love to her, focusing on the turquoise face,
that softness of closed eyes and floating hair.
There, I'll live weightless, breathing water
until one day a wind will come to render me breathless.

Then I'll return, recognize this beach that once felt limitless,
my feet grains of sand rolling beyond sight. Here was the womb
we fell from, when glass turned to release our bodies for an hour,
while our minds built fruits of memory as though they would live forever
— malicious meats below a rose window's monumental light.

What is it that holds us here? In the spring we walk stunned
from ripe, green stalks, leaves and shoots reflected in glassy lagoons
while limbs touch the air behind us. Yet somewhere, clots gather,
attacks of our own blood as we stand atop today's stairs,
yawing above a silence, holding fast to the rail.

What undertow calls us from this sea's forgotten sand?
The mind feels it, asking impossible questions
that glimmer just so only from where we stand.
Yet we feel *something* in that view or we would not look so long
at those clouds pressing to the sea, the light's final collection.

Old Age

Even if the world changes as fast
as the shapes of clouds,
all perfected things at last
fall back to the very old.
— Rilke, "The Sonnets to Orpheus, First Series, No. 19"

I take a step and know no face but the uncertain outline of eternity,
a surenesss of nothing but the mind freed from its hold on my heart.
I walk and look and there is the light of the world — trees that shimmer
with fingers, yet do not hold, frost lifting into a white sky over irrepressible
black writing on water, pines rippling of what is forgotten above.

In Mexico under immovable lintels, I dream of waiting for an earthquake
and am terrified. On a mountain beyond, scars of old mudslides gleam,
surrounded by falling buildings in a morning sun. Below is a green valley,
a white, steepled church in a jungle's violence of yellowing fruit.
This is beauty and despair, memories moving into waking dreams.

Awake, I think of how my mother called me once by her dead husband's name
before she died looking across to Mexico in sea-softened air.
Am I him now and he me? "She was in both worlds, all boundaries falling away,"
my lover said, looking out. Today, across the room, faces grow
indistinct. All that glows comes as reflected water through iced glass.

Now in line at a post office I see clouds billow over green hills outside,
purple deepening winter clouds below a sky's hidden blue. What is matter?
What is thought? Here, my perforated body dims, molecules swimming into air
while Mexico lingers in dreams. Beyond these windows, naked cottonwoods darken
and ravens hover as if to speak. In the distance, snow whitens desireless peaks.

Sleeper

If one took them into intimate sleep and slept deeply
with things — oh how light he'd come
back, changed with change of day, out of mutual depth.
— Rilke, "The Sonnets to Orpheus, Second Series, No. 14"

Now my love sleeps like an angel, I who believe
in no angels but Rilke's barely winged sufficiencies.
How is it to be lapped in this, your only heaven,
remade by sleep into each greening hill's spring
where herds graze by incessant waters?
Yes, it is a dream, but you say all living is a nightmare,
a stone-heavy plain upon your ascendant back.

Awake, you tremble, furious even at trees shimmering
over frozen sidewalks as storms press bright peaks
with tonnage. Awake, you refuse to push the blinds apart,
afraid the day's geese will tumble from mirroring marshes
into a machine noise where matter is never singular.
"How is living in sleep any more deathly than here,"
you ask, "here where variable light ends every thought?"

Is existence less leaden under our sleeping eyes?
Is that silence more vivid, weightless, inexhaustible,
a day's spears of snow across April summits?
Is a quiet florescence all that we would freely bear?
Yet, awake, we move tides around bristling ruins,
reconfigure the shadowing air to build what the mind desires.
Behind closed blinds, the unraveling seems all we can maintain,
the steady lie of the half-open we must break and remake.

Once and Once Only

Be ahead of all departure, as if it were
behind you like the winter that's just passed.
— Rilke, "The Sonnets to Orpheus, Second Series, No. 13"

Why have you loved that death angel so long?
Do you know the full breath of its whistling, final hour?
You who walk beside a poppy's orange petals,
and the bitter cherry's flaming buds with mouthing leaves,
can you remember your child wired and alone on the gurney,
his death wish gasping for a streetlight in the hospital dark?
How much did he swallow before he swam unfailingly back to you?

Once, years ago, I walked beside a yellow dog who looked
only for a hand, never turning back, as ducks buried
their heads in brown water, seeeking only what might be.
Now bedridden, I look out a window at moving pines
in a cold wind even as miles away my son stares again
into life's screen. "There are worlds there," I see him saying to himself,
"if only I wouldn't go crazy watching ravens through the glass."

Behind blinds, I imagine flocks of ravens along our roofline and think
their sudden arrival must be the promise of death
eating our dissolving spirit. Later, I sleep and dream my lungs
have become dried blood. Here, at last, is the image of our malaise,
the transparent angel who is the enemy, our absolute terror,
a diagrammed body whose annunciation none can fight —
the yellow dog, the once-suicidal youth, the moving pines.

Yet isn't there something more? Every day the western snow descends,
clots of white on distant trees, a mountain's undulating spine
remaking still ground. Sleeping, I dream of striding through a slow
encounter between air and earth, a moving, unsettled god
in all that is unchanging, the ground of unseen rain held in a dew
that steams inside with reliable hints of embarkation
where sons and dogs run unfearing into new, unblushable winds.

After the Silence

... the rest is silence.
— Shakespeare, "Hamlet"

Silent friend of many distances,
feel how your breath is still expanding space.
— Rilke, "The Sonnets to Orpheus, Second Series, No. 29"

After his incandescence of words, what could he have heard
on those ramparts beyond a father lost and mother faithless
that could recall his avenging angel?
What could he, the reluctant killer, do at last but step across?
Every hour I look into water and see a suggestion
of the eternal, matter's curving calligraphy
in changing convections of light.
This is the painting I might have chosen if I could have, too,
strands where clouds stream purple
and the heart plays only to longings of imagination.
There, walking over sand in a play larger
than any god I could imagine, I might have created
my own future, timeless afternoons on a beach,
an iridescence of weighty promises.

But would it have been enough, that forever palpable beach
with its persistent, friendly, impermeable air?
Or would it have been just a bell unable to speak with vapors,
its feet unencompassed by the beat of equinoxes?
Would there have been only that steady airlessness of memory
along a strand, where now the hour my mother smiled across
the dinner table becomes an illusion, reminding me
of a dimming sky and another body gone like that spent noon
my father drove away in tropical quiet
and never came back. After that hour, nothing but a fading,
circumstantial overcast from a sea subsumimg all,
nightly easings of breath to ward off belief,
interminable waves rolling through irredeemable fish.

Yet behind that beach, cliffs carry green recollections,
inconsequential streams that feed this faithless ocean,
footworn rocks along a bushy shore shaped by longing.
Here the mind sleeps and he sleeps, too, the avenged Dane
made still amid sounds or currents that count their differences.
Here the living veins run wide and full or narrow and weak
into waiting cups. Here, kicking froths fly from channels
resistant to change while slow undertones raise
small lives squeezed out of rock. And beyond,
only the half-believed — an unpondered breath
unsought for what it might be — a consolable susurration
of ripening flesh, the slow ladder of a common climbing
the certain, glimpsed oblivion of imagined seas,
if it be not now, yet it will come, our last and deepest love.

A Silent World

Behind this one it breathes
through flesh less tangible than air,
rising from dying grass into shadow rivers
and the silent tongues of clouds.
At times it is an immensity of sand
under lines of cormorants,
at others the blurred ground of a forest
where steps dissolve into roots
and snow lifts against stone.
Desire will not bring it, only this letting go —
silhouetted trees reaching for spectral crows
with hints of an appearance, a rustle
through quiet fields in January hills
where wild roses carry the scent of pears
across waters unseen and unheard,
the mute undertow of another earth.

Imagination

Love, the World exists nowhere but within.
Our life is lived in transformation. And diminishing,
the outer world vanishes.
— Rilke, "The Seventh Elegy"

In this World, the soil is red and the day
never ends with the same horizon.
I walk among ocotillo and saguaro
knowing water is illusion, but drink easily.
Every rock is a kaleidoscope under a sun
that rises and sets at any time of day.
Clouds are often purple even at noon
and when it rains, canyons release
soils in crimson streams
as a lizard snatches insects in its tongue
without eating them.

No one goes hungry or dies here without wishing it.
There is no illness except Kierkegaard's
"sickness unto death" and that soon passes.
Turquoise is the most valuable gem,
but no one is obsessed with it, so it's free.
There is pain, yes, but only the pain
of desiring what can't be summoned.
Rocks alone speak and then
only in colors — yellows and scarlets,
all of them sounding out in my head
as a dreaming, silent orchestra.

This is no paradise and will never be. All trees are junipers
yielding only small blue fruit and little shade.
This is *my* afterlife — somewhat like the world I lived in,
but a little better — more light-filled, open,
smelling of sage and possible rain.
I can see it's only a start — that now all *is* possible —
ice forests, the liquid plains, the airless planets
with transient creatures flying under blue stars,
all of them known to me as I make them, after waiting so long.

In the Moment in a Dark Wood

It comes suddenly after a dinner with friends,
an unidentifiable road past unfamiliar houses,
rolling from porchlight to porchlight
through fog or fluorescent night,
guiding you to a corner of your last dream —
the big pine, the vacant gas station by the weedy field,
an intersection where you might turn and feel grounded,

even as it fades, leaving your past behind.
Above, the light is red; to the right, a ghostly freeway;
to the left an idea of home beyond blurred signs,
sidewalks you may have grown up on,
an open room under a streetlamp,
a bed surrounded by trees
beside a waterless pool.

A choice, then. For hours you sit at the light
in a dark chill over the humming engine and dream;
there is no rush. How good to be free;
everything ahead is a decision.
There's nothing to hold you,
nothing to remember.
All you can lose is your life.

Notes

AT FORT ROCK, Page 46

In 1938 a cache of sandals was found in a cave near present-day Fort Rock State Park, Oregon. The sandals have been dated to a least 9,000 years ago, testifying to human habitation in what is now desert during a time when it was a place of grassland, lakes, and pockets of woodland.

DEATH OF THE ICEMAN, Page 49

In 1991, the frozen body of a man who lived 5,300 years ago during the Neolithic age emerged from a melting glacier in Italy. A study of the remains found an arrowhead in his back. New information released in 2011 indicates he died from a combination of the arrow wound and blunt-force trauma, both apparently suffered in an ambush.

THE YDE GIRL, Page 50

Some 1,800 bodies from the Bronze Age have been found preserved in bogs in Great Britain, Denmark, and Holland. Many show signs of violence, their throats cut before they were apparently cast into the bog. Some experts theorize they were sacrifices to gods in hard times when harvests were lean; others say they may have been criminals executed for misdeeds. No one knows, as they left no written records.

DETAILS ON ARTWORK BY DON GRAY

Cover Art: "Loom of the Land," acrylic on canvas, 48" X 36," copyright 2005 Don Gray, *www.dongraystudio.com*

Title page: "Heaven and Earth #3," charcoal on two sheets paper, 44" X 26," 2010

Pg. 11: "Food Chain," charcoal and pencil on paper, 14" X 16.5," completed 12/11/11

Pg. 37: "Flyover," charcoal and pencil on paper, 14" X 16.5," completed 12/10/11

Pg. 63: "The Memory of Moisture," charcoal and pencil on paper, 14" X 16.5," completed 12/13/11

Pg. 85: "Season's Lament," charcoal and pencil on paper, 14" X 16.5," completed 12/12/11

About Steve Dieffenbacher

Steve Dieffenbacher has lived in Oregon's Rogue Valley since 1989. His poem "Emptiness" won the 2010 poetry prize sponsored by *Cloudbank* magazine of Corvallis, Oregon, and he has been published in numerous regional journals. His poems also are included in *Deer Drink the Moon* (2007), an anthology of Oregon poetry published by Ooligan Press at Portland State University; in the chapbooks *Universe of the Unsaid* (2009), *Voices of the Siskiyous* (2006), and *At the Boundary* (2001); in the anthology *Intricate Homeland: Collected Writings from the Klamath Siskiyou* (2000); and in *A Path Through Stone,* a 1995 cycle of poems that includes work by Bruce Barton, Jonah Bornstein and John Reid. He is an editor at the *Mail Tribune* in Medford, where he writes a monthly column focusing on nature and hiking for the newspaper's Sunday travel section. He has won various awards for writing, photography, and page design in his more than 35 years as a journalist.

CPSIA information can be obtained at www.ICGtesting.com
Printed in the USA
LVOW130221100512

281138LV00003B/15/P

9 781877 655753